"And if a player I have coached can say to himself honestly that he **gave** the **best** that was in him, then he's learned something a lot more important than winning.

"He's learned **how** to win."

# "interviews"

# An Interview with
# bobby knight

## By Larry Batson
## Photographs by Rich Clarkson

CREATIVE EDUCATION/CHILDRENS PRESS

Published by Creative Educational Society, Inc., 123 South Broad Street,
Mankato, Minnesota 56001. Copyright © 1977 by Creative Educational
Society, Inc. International copyrights reserved in all countries. No part of this
book may be reproduced in any form without written permission from the
publisher. Printed in the United States.

Library of Congress Cataloging in Publication Data

Batson, Larry, 1930-
  Bobby Knight.

   SUMMARY: A biography of the basketball coach at the University of
Indiana, whose undefeated team won the NCAA tournament in 1976.
   1. Knight, Bobby—Juvenile literature. 2. Basketball coaches—United
States—Biography—Juvenile literature. [1. Knight, Bobby. 2. Basketball
coaches] I. Title.
GV884.K58B37     796.32'3'0924 [B] [92]      76-42271
ISBN 0-87191-574-X

Success isn't making a lot of money or covering your walls with trophies or getting your name in the newspapers and your picture on television, Bobby Knight was saying. It's none of those things.

"Success is performing to the limit of your potential," he said. "It's trying your level best so that you can look back and say to yourself, 'I did everything I possibly could.'

"None of us ever quite get there. But we can try, by golly, we can try. And if a player I have coached can say to himself honestly that he gave the best that was in him, then he's learned something a lot more important than winning. He's learned how to win.

"There's a heck of a lot of difference. Winning is great. It's a wonderful feeling — the whole world is yours. But it only only lasts a little while. What stays with you is knowing what it takes to play to the best of your potential."

Knight knows about winning . . . and losing. He's the basketball coach at the University of Indiana and his team had just completed an undefeated season by winning the national major college championship. His Hoosiers had beaten Michigan

86 to 68 in the finals of the NCAA tournament a month earlier.

Now Knight was sprawled in a chair in an airport restaurant sipping a glass of orange juice and Seven-Up. They don't make chairs big enough for Knight, or at least they don't put them in airport restaurants.

He is a big man, about 6-feet, 4-inches, with broad shoulders and chest and long arms and legs. He has a bold prow of a nose, dark, deep-set eyes under heavy brows and dark, wavy hair with a touch of gray. He's 36 but he doesn't look that old. He was a basketball player for Ohio State University in the early 1960's — not a great one but pretty good — and he's not much above playing weight now.

Lolling in that chair, talking and laughing with an old friend who had met his plane, Knight looked for all the world like a big collie pup who had flopped on a lawn after a romp. Not tired, ready to go again any time.

"Let me tell you something about losing," he said. "It might give you an idea of how long a winner's reputation lasts.

"Last year our team won 31 games and lost one —
to Kentucky in the NCAA regionals. Now that's
pretty good, isn't it?

"Well, the morning after that Kentucky game, I
went down to a drugstore to buy a newspaper.
This fellow came up to me. I'd never seen him
before and haven't seen him since. I really don't
care if I never see him again.

"Anyway, he took me by the arm and said,
'Coach, I just want you to know that I'm still with
you.'

"Now what can you say after a remark like that? I
looked at him for a second and said, 'Buddy, I'm
just darned glad we didn't lose two games this
year.' "

Knight speaks bluntly. Sometimes his frankness
jars listeners. But in the long run, they appreciate it.
When he is displeased with a player, it boils out like
a thunderstorm and afterward the air is clear again.

Players have told of a plane trip home after Indiana
lost a game. Knight sat up front going over the
game, analyzing what went wrong. He decided that

"Winning is great… What stays with you is knowing what it takes to **play** to the best of your potential."

a senior on the squad had failed to take charge when he should have.

He roared out the player's name and the player, who was half-asleep, tried to leap to his feet without unfastening his seatbelt. It took him a while to get untangled and then Coach Knight spent several minutes chewing him out royally.

A few days later, two other players were talking of the incident.

"Man, I thought we were all going to get a piece of that," said one.

"So did I," said a freshman, "and I was just hoping he was going by class."

Knight will push his players. Sometimes he'll yell at them and they'll resent it, says Mike Krzyzewski, who played for him at West Point, the United States Military Academy. "But overall, you're going to love the experience of playing for him. You're going to appreciate his honesty. He'll never lie to you."

In 1969 Krzyzewski was the captain of the West Point team. The Cadets had two important games coming up. They had to win both to be invited to the National Invitational Tournament.

Krzyzewski's father died suddenly and Knight drove his player to the airport to catch a plane home to Chicago. The next day Knight — who normally never lets anything interfere with his team's practices — flew to Chicago himself. He visited the family, went to the funeral, and told Krzyzewski to spend as much time as he needed with his mother.

"He was a young coach as I am now," Krzyzewski said, "and I know how much getting into the NIT meant to him. It was the dream of every Army team.

"But he never said a word about missing those practices himself and he told me not to worry about anything but my mom. As it happened, I got back just in time to leave on the trip. We played Friday and Saturday night, won both games and went to the tournament.

"He never said a word about that to anybody," said Krzyzewski, who is now coach at West Point himself. "Later on when I joined him as an assistant at Indiana, nobody on the staff there knew about it. Coach Knight always calls my mom when he goes through Chicago and sees that she has game tickets when Indiana plays there. And nobody knew a thing about it until I told them.''

Knight doesn't talk about himself. He'll talk about basketball or his players, about golf or fishing or country music. He'll talk about the people he admires and why, but he fidgets and growls and changes the subject when asked about himself.

"I'd be just as happy," he said, "if I never had my name in the paper or my picture on TV. Let 'em write about the games and the players. I'd be satisified if they would just wait until I die and carve on my tombstone, 'He was his own man — and he was honest.' ''

Name some people you admire, Knight was asked, and tell us why.

"From athletics, John Havlicek — for competitiveness; Pete Rose — for hustle; Ted Williams — for dedication. My favorite politician was Harry Truman.

"Each, in some way, stood for something important. Each one epitomizes some quality. Every one of them worked as hard as anybody possibly could to reach his potential. Every one of

them maintained the same set of principles through good times and rough ones.

"There are so many great stories about Truman. He never backed down from anything and he had a pretty good set of priorities. I about died laughing when I read his reason for firing General MacArthur because the general wouldn't respect the authority of the President: 'I didn't fire him because he was a dumb blankety-blank, although he was, but that's not against the law for generals.'

> "Every one of them maintained the same set of principles through good times and rough ones."

"I remember reading where somebody asked Williams what he wanted out of baseball. He told them, 'I want to walk down the street and have people say there goes the greatest hitter who ever lived.'

"Nobody ever tried harder every day, every play than Rose.

"John Havlicek and I played together at Ohio State. Knowing him is one of the great good twists of fortune in my life, and there have been a few.

"He's the greatest basketball player who ever lived. And he's never let that spoil him. He's the same man I knew in college.

"When we were getting ready to play Michigan (for the 1976 national championship), he talked to our team. He didn't once mention winning. He didn't mention the national championship.

"He said something like, 'Fellows, when you go out there tonight, you're going to be involved in a

basketball game for two hours that you're going to remember for a long, long time. When the time comes to think back on it, what's important is to be able to tell yourselves in all truth that you did the very best you could . . . whatever happens in that game is insignificant as opposed to that.' "

The lessons Knight tries to teach his players are ones he learned himself as an athlete and, later, coming up through the ranks of coaching. None of the lessons came easy.

He was a high school star in football, basketball, and baseball at Orrville, Ohio, a town of about 8,500 population. But at Ohio State, he started only a few games. He hated sitting on the bench, but says now that it probably made him a better coach.

"If I were good enough, I'd still be playing," he said, "like Havlicek. but if you aren't good enough and love sports, there's just one road left — into coaching.

"A coach's perspective and a player's are worlds apart. And a great athlete can have problems adjusting to coaching. For some of them, things come far too easily. They have a hard time understanding that by far the vast majority of players are just average athletes.

"Leaders aren't necessarily people with super gifts. They are ordinary people with extraordinary determination. The same is true of a lot of athletes that are successful. A coach has to understand that.

"You know the hardest single thing for a player to learn?

It's **concentration**."

"You hear people say that some schools win all the time because they get great talent. Actually talent is pretty evenly distributed. What people make of their own talent is the most important factor.

"Take Kent Benson (Indiana's All-American center). He comes to the forefront, after a lot of hard work, and people start saying he's a brilliant natural talent. Not really. He just worked harder to improve himself than did some others with equal talent.

"You know the hardest single thing for a player to learn? It's concentration.

"Test yourself. See how hard it is to keep your mind on one thing. We're talking, but there are people walking by, conversations at the tables around us, planes taking off. Try to blot those out entirely and concentrate on our conversation. You can't do it, not entirely."

Knight's practices are focussed on improving his players' concentration.

"Leaders
aren't necessarily
people with
super gifts.

They are
ordinary
people..."

"There is no right way to play basketball," he said, no single, inflexible style or system. "But there are a lot of wrong ways."

"We work within a certain framework to eliminate the wrong ways," he said. Indiana players learn certain rules — dribble as little as possible, don't make two consecutive cuts in the same direction, things like that — which are designed to keep the players from making mistakes.

The result is that Knight's players almost always make the right moves, swiftly, surely, without hesitation. When it is attacking, an Indiana team moves downcourt with a series of lightning-like passes, probing the opponent's defense, putting pressure on the weak spots and eventually cracking it open.

The Hoosiers play a tigerish man-to-man defense. They apply pressure far down the court and try to force opponents into mistakes or into taking bad shots.

Either way, an Indiana player must concentrate. Knight teaches that. There is another necessary quality which Knight looks for when he recruits athletes. That is cooperation. A player who doesn't like to give up the basketball can't play for Indiana.

"Really we pay more attention to a player's personality than to his talent when we're recruiting," Knight said. "We try to get an athlete who will fit in with what we're doing and with our players. Then we'll match his basketball skills with whatever we've got going."

Knight has one rule of behavior for players: "If you do anything that reflects badly on the university or the team, I will take whatever action is appropriate."

Indiana players are expected to dress neatly, to stay out of beer joints and other trouble spots, and, in general, to present a good image. They must keep their hair trimmed. It doesn't have to be short, but it can't be in their eyes or on their shoulders; not during the season.

"Short hair, long hair — I don't care about it," said Knight. "Lordy, when I was in high school we all had crewcuts with our scalp showing through on top. Looked liked a bunch of skunks. I hope we never get back to that. But it's a matter of team togetherness, of cooperation and closeness."

Knight demands a lot of his players. He works them hard. They play his way or not at all. But he

"But if you aren't good enough and **love** sports, there's just one road left – into **coaching.**"

trusts them and he gives them more responsibility than many coaches do.

There was a game in which Kansas led Indiana by one point with 40 seconds left in an overtime period. Guard John Laskowski was bringing the ball up the court. He looked to his bench for instructions.

At a time like that, nine coaches out of 10 would call for a time-out. "I mean, there are a lot of possibilities," Laskowski said later. "Do you want to play for one shot? Do you want to take the first shot we get? Do you want to work for a layup?"

Knight just waved his his hand and hollered, "Let's go."

Laskowski drove up the court, cut between two Kansas players and sank a 12-foot jump shot.

Many coaches hover near their players after games, making sure they say the proper thing to the writers who swarm into the locker room. Knight leaves the room and lets his players talk freely.

Most important of all, when his own future is on the line, Knight lets his players have the final say on recruiting.

"Really we pay
more attention
to a player's
personality
than to his talent
when we're
recruiting."

The head coach and his assistants scout high school players throughout the season. They go to games, look at films, talk to coaches. Then they invite a few prospects to visit the campus.

"When a guy visits us, our players take over," Knight said. "All of the team, not just one or two. They show the prospect around. They really try to get to know him.

"Then they tell me what they think. If they tell me they don't think a kid will fit in, that's the end of it. He doesn't get a scholarship.

"It's their team. I'm not going to put on it somebody they don't want to play with."

Knight has obviously got his beliefs across to his team. Although you don't go through two seasons of competition, including national tournament play, with only one loss with untalented players, you can't achieve such a record without the cooperation of all your players.

# creative education

# "interviews"